LET THE TRUTH BE TOLD II
Confessions

Copyright © 2010 Shawna M. Harrison

Published by HER TRU SOUL PUBLISHING

All rights reserved. Except for use in the case of brief quotations embodied in critical articles and reviews, the reproduction or utilization of this work in whole or part in any form by any electronic, digital, mechanical or other means, now known or hereafter invented, including xerography, photocopying, scanning, recording, or any information storage or retrieval system, is forbidden without prior written permission of the author and publisher.
The scanning, uploading, and distribution of this book via the Internet or via any other means without permission of the publisher and author is illegal and punishable by law. Purchase only authorized versions of this book and do not participate in or encourage electronic piracy of copyrighted materials. Your support of the author's rights is appreciated.
Names, characters, places, and incidents are based on the author's own personal experience therefore names of persons and entities remain unnamed to protect the integrity of the story and the privacy of those involved. Any group or organization listed is for informational purposes only and does not imply endorsement or support of their activities or organization.

For ordering, booking, permission, or questions, contact the author.

ISBN: 978-0-578-07291-3

Printed in the United States of America
First Printing 2010

Edited by: HER TRU SOUL PUBLISHING
Illustrations by: Darrell Gilbert email: dgart9201@yahoo.com

LTBT II-CONFESSIONS

Dedication

I am very pleased and grateful to have had the opportunity to share in the lives of these women. I thank the women for sharing their love and appreciation for me, verbally, emotionally and publicly. I am also grateful to those women that chose not to share their inner most feelings, I do understand, there is no love lost. Some of these women I've only known for a short while but then there are others that I have known or known me most of my life. All of these women have impacted my world, some small, some great. They all have played a part in me becoming the woman that I am today. Ladies I would like to apologize to you for hurting you in any way. Please find it within yourself to forgive me. I will always be here for you as a true and compassionate friend. I love you dearly.

LTTBT II-CONFESSIONS

LTBT II-CONFESSIONS

Confession #1

Kay, an old friend of ours, called me Saturday night to remind me I had agreed to join her, and a friend, in from Nashville out that evening. I asked, "What time ?" We decided on 11. It was around 8. I would not be on time. I arrived at Kay's place a little after 11, dressed in a disobedient button down shirt that refused to stay closed and a brown vest that kept some of the buttons from freeing themselves. Kay met me half dressed at the door. I walked in and looked around the house.

There I met Shawna.

She was short but she had this powerful stance. Dressed in bold colors. Kay introduced us. She kept calling me ma'am. I knew she wasn't young enough to think I was that much older than she was. But her voice was distinct. It commanded attention more than the colors, hats, stance.... the voice forced you to take notice. Kay and I made small talk as they got ready. I walked throughout the apartment taking notice of all the new decorations in the place. It looked more like a home than my first visit there.

As we walked out, Kay asked me "So what do YOU think about Shawna !?!" Kay was hopeful. I was emotionally unavailable but definitely not blind. "She's cute," I replied casually, taking another sip from my drink. We all jumped in the truck and Kay left us for a moment to retrieve something from the apartment.

Shawna began to do something most women are hesitant to do with me. She peppered me with a round of questions. Her anxiety made me calm. We looked at pictures from the day she and Kay had spent. Then Letoya Luckett's cd came on. She asked whether or not I was familiar with it. "What's your favorite song on here ?" " I told her, 'I cant remember the number but I think its 6. good to me." She wanted to know why that one. I told her "because of the lyrics. Its so simple & well written. I mean that's all I want, just be good to me." Kay entered the vehicle and immediately changed the song. Shawna told her to hold up, "that's J's favorite song." Kay said, "that girl ain't got no favorite song."

We drove downtown. They told me stories about the 3 musketeers. A group made up of Shawna, Kay & Alvin . They had some wild experiences between them. Kay's girlfriend came up in conversation. She was not a fan of mine. I made mention of her sour attitude. Kay got defensive. So conversation ended, until a pretty girl in a club window waved at Kay. We went in long enough to find out the girl was feeling sassy enough to draw a woman's attention, but not enough to entertain her. From there we went to another club. Shawna spoke to everyone. It seemed everyone was at least an acquaintance. She even got some beads from the doorman.

We got in line to check coats. Shawna kept us there a little too long explaining the importance of her ostrich skin jacket. As lovely as it was, it was not going to be any more important to the coat check girl. I pulled her along into the elevator and up to the dance floor. It was jam packed on the 2nd floor. The room was full of thirsty men, half dressed women, freaks touching their toes and few professionals.

Kay bought the first round of drinks. As we made a move through the crowd a man decided Shawna's behind was something he could not resist touching. She looked at me. I pointed at the guilty party. She grabbed me and said "You've got to watch out for me." I said, "okay." Four feet from the last one, a short, stout, bald black man grabbed Shawna's hand and began to make conversation. Kay was oblivious. I grabbed Shawna's hand to move us forward and to keep all of us together. She smiled like I had hung the moon.

We moved over to a corner of the dance floor, stood, and took the first round of pictures. Shawna and I danced some. The overwhelming energy in the club took away any desire, I had to be there, soon after arriving. I took up a conversation with an older, Italian gentleman who bought me drinks all evening. This made me the envy of several black men, some made their feelings known. I was amused because I knew the time between us would end on the 2nd floor of this dance club.

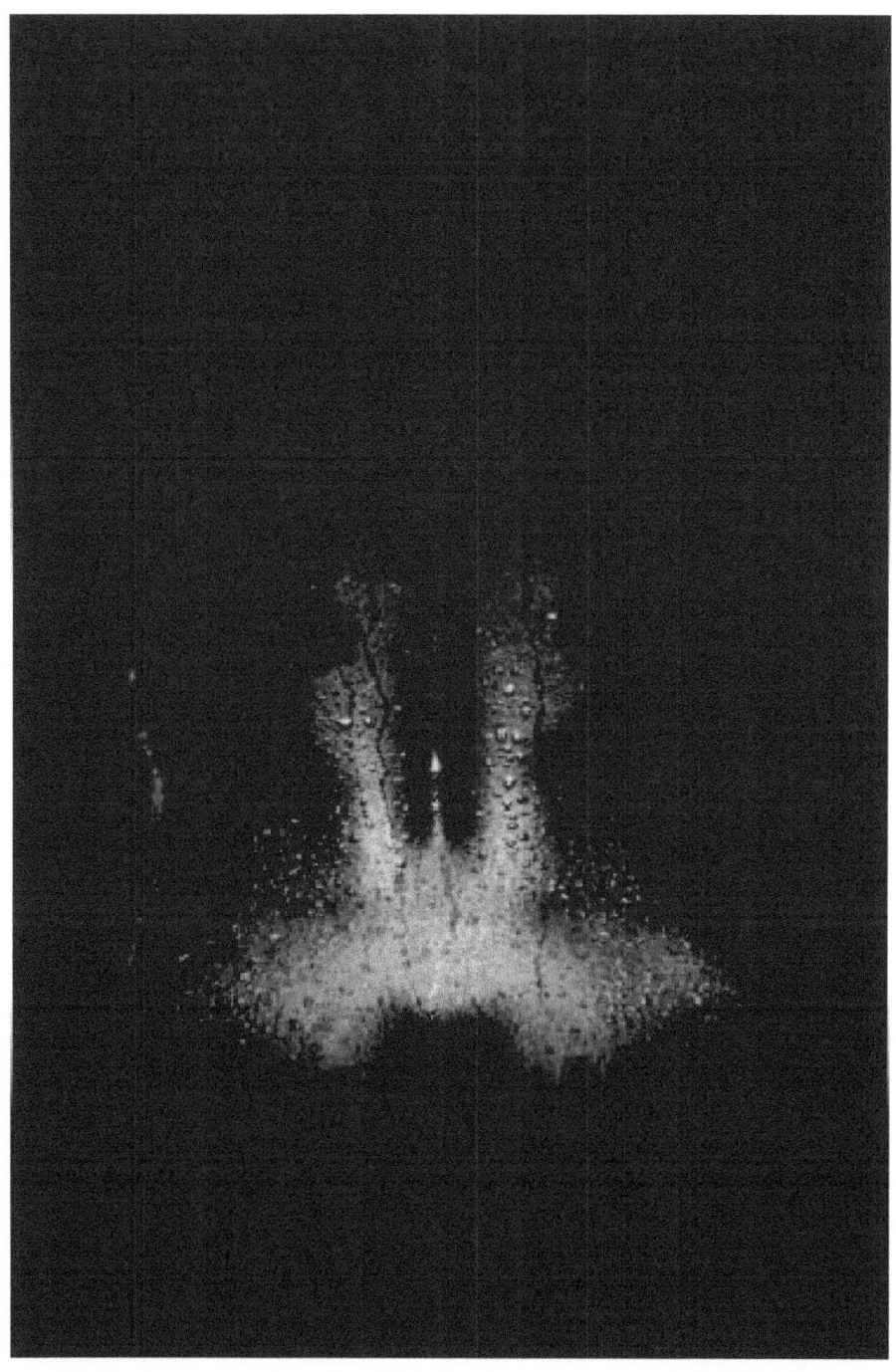

Drinks flowed, the girls tore the dance floor up, even involving me by pulling me in to dance in a three part performance near the bar I was standing at. The men stared, rubbing their crotches, pointing to their boys and back at the one they were most fascinated with. After that song, Shawna took my hand, gave me "the face," and a tug toward the dance floor, "I wanna dance with you." I was not moved. I told her "go dance with Kay, have fun." Time passed Kay and Shawna found some "good time girls" to dance with. I was happy for them. I played wing-man for the Italian fellows friend. Then returned to our conversation.

Soon enough the club was close to closing. As the second floor emptied, we took our party down to the first floor. Where a few more dances were had, until I was called over to make my exit.

I was in a mood to be close so I asked Shawna to sit in the back with me. She curled up in my lap and promptly fell asleep. We all went upstairs to the apartment. Kay said we could play the Wii. I was so over this hot wig I wearing. We were all drunk, tired and ready for the night to end. But Shawna entered the room with her shirt unbuttoned. My eyes drifted over her breasts, the brightly colored bra and the tattoo over her belly button. The power she emanated earlier grew. She was illuminating. She walked up to me, made slight movements toward my face, my lips. I didn't move but I knew I didn't want to kiss her then. I noticed the scratches on her forearm. I held her right arm and asked
"What happened here ?"
She said "It's a long story."
I said "I've got time."
She said "No you don't."
Shawna left the room to find me a rubber band. When she returned, she made an attempt to put it on. I felt my wig slip and poof it was gone. I began to laugh, she said "J, it should be on more secure than that, shouldn't it ?" I laughed and said "It was." We all tried to make conversation. Kay's girlfriend came in. Suddenly Shawna was very aware that her shirt was open. She clutched it closed. I giggled.

We all made conversation for a little while. A local church service was broadcast on TV One. Shawna whispered to me "spend the night. I'll wash

your clothes. I'll iron them stay." "We can go to church in the morning." I smiled and told her no. "I want to go home to my own bed." Shawna curled up on the couch next to me, rested her head in my thigh and went to sleep.
Kay and Dan walked off to their bedroom. I motioned to Kay, about Shawna on my lap, like what am I supposed to do. Kay shrugged her shoulders and continued walking. I stroked Shawna's arm.... cheek ...hair to get her up. She walked me out to my car. Where we sat talking about the evening. She asked me what was the worst part of the evening. Then I asked hers, she told me when I came in I, "you were so quiet, you didn't say much.' "I have to survey everything first. Once I'm comfortable I'll speak." Soon she fell asleep again. I watched her sleep for a while. It was almost 8 in the morning, a long drive was ahead of me. So I caressed her cheek until she woke up. I told her "I've got to go." We hugged and parted ways.

I didn't hear from Shawna until she sent an apology through Kay's phone for "her behavior." I asked what that meant, she just repeated herself. I accepted. Kay called me a few days later. She made idle conversation for a few minutes and then told me Shawna wanted to talk to me. Her voice came booming through the phone. "What's up J-boog !?" I couldn't help but to smile. We spoke for a short time until Kay said she would put the phone down and let us talk. Which we did.

The next week Shawna and I spoke daily. She talked a lot about what seems to keep her grounded. She spoke with such conviction when it came to her purpose, to raise her son Shawn and to write. I admired her dedication. A rare and beautiful thing to find. She was a Cancer, like my father. He's my favorite guy and the quintessential Cancer. Shawna had this easy ability to include me in future plans. Always in a playful mood despite the time or what commitment was next.

She gave me the opportunity to check out her website. There I read her story. We shared some similar unfortunate occurrences in our childhood. But to meet her, you would never know how far she has come. No matter how small my doubt was, she was encouraging. I suppose this is why I noticed that light around her. The first week we spoke, I was having a lot of nightmares. I told her my nights were rough. I never told her this, but I wonder is there something in the water in Nashville. Despite her numerous commitments, she offered me time. She said, "call me whenever, we can talk until you feel better." I was stunned by her kindness. In a time when everyone is in a "recession" mindset with money, time, kindness and whatever that can be shared. She was always sure to extend herself to me. There was some hope we would get closer. I was uncertain. A recent break-up had left me splintered. Thankfully she didn't press me for anything more than friendship. I was grateful. It gave me a greater respect for her level of maturity, her entry into my life is truly a pleasure. She came to restore my faith. There are in fact several exceptional women still here, ready to love, again.

LTBT II-CONFESSIONS

Confession #2

When Shawna first asked me to write "our" story, I didn't know quite how to approach it. Shawna and I have been knowing each other for some years, but there has never been an "us",
a "potential us",
a "maybe it could be us"
or even a "promising us"
but never an "us".
So I didn't know exactly how to tell a story that was never "our" story, but here goes..........

I met Shawna on a breezy fall night in October, 2004. It was one of my first times out in a Nashville Gay club. A couple of friends of mine talked me into going out and I really wasn't into clubbing, but I was trying to get out and meet other people "in the life". I noticed her earlier that night in the club, beyond her being the sexy little thing that she is, she was also the loudest, boisterous person in the club. I was amazed at how the shortest smallest thing could seem as though she was wearing a microphone...lol.

She had a amazing laugh and seemed to be very easy going. And yes, I got this from just watching her in the club. You see I'm a people watcher and for me its cool to just watch people interact in their element.

So moving on, I actually meet her when I was leaving the club. She was leaving as I was leaving, and for those that know Shawna knows that she will strike up a conversation with anyone! After she talked with my very flamboyant male friend for a while, we introduced ourselves. After a few "I have never seen you out" and laughs, we exchanged numbers and promises to call soon.

After about a week and no call, I figured I wouldn't hear from her, and chopped it up to a "drunk" club night. Yes, I could have called her, but I was involved with someone long distance that was on again/off again who was in Arizona for school. Call it crazy, but it felt less like infidelity if I wasn't the one to make the initial call. So nevertheless I was shocked when she called the next day. We exchanged the getting to know you pleasantries and agreed to go out the following week.

My first "sober" impression of Shawna when we actually did go out was she was still indeed a sexy little thing. And I keep saying "little" because I am 5'10" and have never dated someone so much shorter than I, but it was cool and new. So I was okay with it. She was very confident to say the least and spoke in 3rd person a lot. Which was cute, but a little arrogant. We had a great time though from what I recall. We never really had any issues, but I do remember her going through my phone and calling the girl I was dealing with in AZ to introduce herself as my "friend" Shawna. She was wild and always had to make her presence known.

We went out a few more times and I met her handsome nephew, even hung out at her crib. I really liked Shawna, but it seems like she was always just out of reach. When we first started hanging out, she gave me a schedule of her available days (wtf?).
It was wild, she actually had days out of the week that she wasn't available and days that could be our date days. The honesty was refreshing but brutal at best.
I always felt like I couldn't give her what she needed and she would never give me what I needed. So I limited myself and my time with her. We hugged a few times, kissed a few more, but I wouldn't put myself in a position for any real intimacy with her. I honestly think that is what she found appealing in me, that's what kept her attraction to me. I kept my distance and didn't throw myself at her like I seen so many women (and men for that matter) do.

She oozed sexiness, but I wanted more than that and maybe she could have given me more, but honestly I never gave her a real chance too. We both knew from the beginning what we had or was building up to wasn't and wouldn't be exclusive.
And that was okay for both of us.

I have had a few relationships and I assume she has too, but we have always kept in touch. Until I got into a serious relationship and got married, I have always flirted with the idea of an "us". Always had a shred of hope that maybe, one day we could be what each other needed in a mate, but it never came to pass. We have both had our share of bullshitting each other, but thankfully we have remained friends over the years.

And in the broad spectrum of life, I guess that is all that really matters in the end.

LTTBT II-CONFESSIONS

Confession #3

Little did I know that my life was going to change August 2003. I just got back from training and was headed back to work at Dell. I was doing my job like usual and this short, light skinned female caught my eye. I completely stopped everything I was doing and watched her walk pass, not even thinking she would look back but she did. I couldn't believe it she caught me staring, I was so embarrassed.

Our first break came along so I went in the break room and sat by myself and to my surprise she walked over and introduced herself to me and invited me to sit with her and her friends. I was speechless I didn't know what to say. We spoke for the rest of the break then she invited me to go to lunch with them. So here we are riding in the back seat to lunch, we get our food and she insists on putting my napkin in my lap and fixing my food for me. All I kept thinking was, "is this really happening", I'd never been catered to like that before .

That evening after work we sat by our cars and talked, intrigued by each other wanting to know more and more about each other. Our first time hanging outside of work I went to her house and she washed my hair for me, after that I was over her house almost every night.

Two months later, I was moving my stuff in. Mind you this was my first real relationship, so everything I was experiencing was new to me and a wonderful thing. I would come home from a long day at work and she would have rose petals leading throughout the house, candles lit, a hot bath ran, and dinner made. She took me to places I had never been before, Gatlinburg was my favorite and the most romantic. We went during the winter time, it was a surprise all the way until we got there. This was my first time ever going to Gatlinburg and staying in a chalet. It was perfect, I couldn't have asked for more.

We didn't have to go out and do things to enjoy each other, we would spend our days off cuddled up on the couch playing video games and watching TV.

She always made holidays very special and surprising, I could never imagine what she would have in store for me. I can honestly say like Tyler Perry quoted, "people come into our lives as roots, branches, and leaves", she has been a very strong root in my life. I am very thankful and grateful to have had the opportunity to have her in my life.

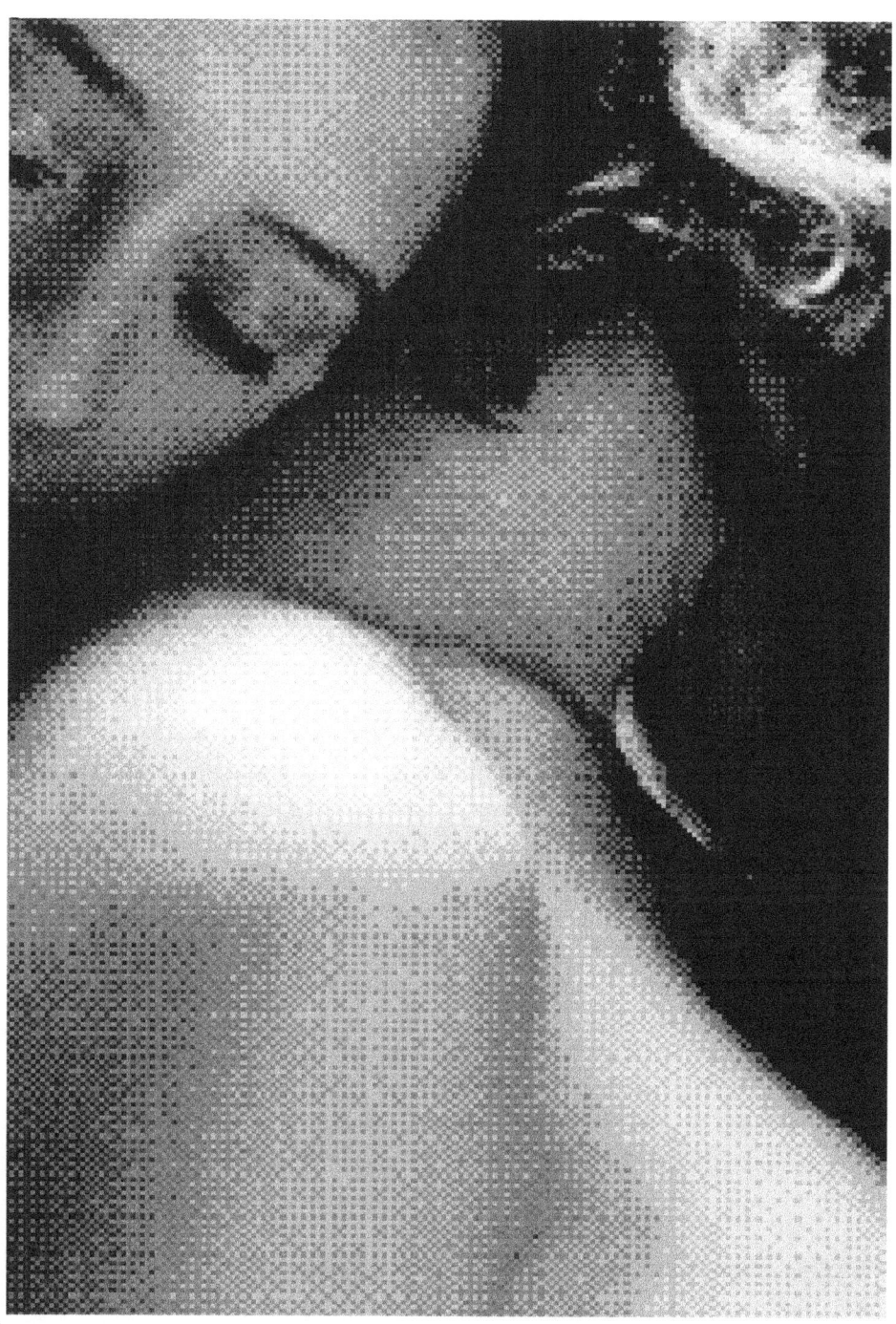

Confession #4

In my first non business conversation with Shawna, we clicked like old friends. Like vintage jewelry the road we were about to travel was expensive yet worthwhile in the lessons we learned.

I was on my way out of town, not willing to surrender to boredom when I decided to read a rough draft of something she wrote. Having a similar childhood background is what drew me to read her story...It was an unforgettable two hours...as I read it was almost like I felt what she felt not to the same degree, however her writing was just that compelling. While reading I caught myself trying to saddle rope my emotions into submission and they just wouldn't comply. Have you ever watched a movie where the dam was about to crack? Well that's what I was like trying to read what she wrote, sitting on the train holding back the flood.

I met Shawna through work and we had only communicated as needed, but on this day after reading I wanted to know more about her life, her story left me with more questions. I wanted to wrap my arms around her sadness and tell her that everything would be okay. Its not that I routinely live vicariously through others but in this one moment I wanted her to act like she was on a talk show and tell me all the things that made her happy and all the things that made her sad.

So I called her. And she answered.

I didn't know what to expect because all my dealings with her prior were on a professional level. I explained to her that I had just read her rough draft and we talked a bit about what I thought of her writing and I told her that I had questions. She welcomed my questions, her excitement about sharing her story was refreshing. So we talked for the rest of the day into the night. Minutes became hours as she answered every question I had, even the painful ones.

From this day long telephone call I felt endeared to her, because she opened up to me, a practical stranger. And I was immediately impressed with her honesty and transparency.

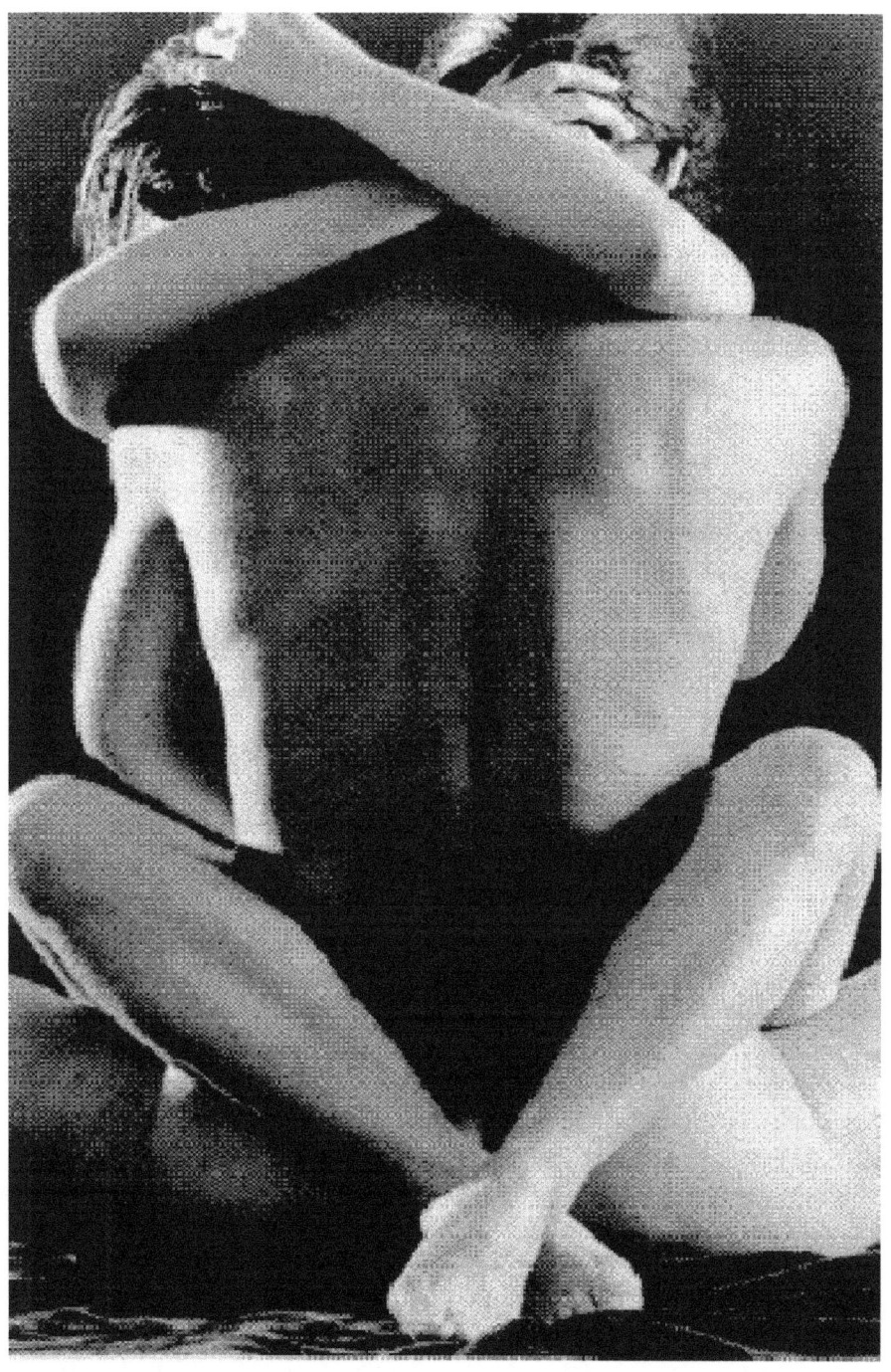

In our conversation I quickly realized that her emotions were still very tender and that I should be careful with her heart...and even on the next day after our long conversation I caught myself wondering, "Is she okay?" I was wondering this because answering my questions had caused her to relive painful things and I knew by the end of our conversation that day that she was upset. I felt helpless and although my relationship with God at the time was lukewarm I sought His help for her, I asked Him to be there for her because I did not yet know how to. I sent her a text and eventually we talked and she explained to me that even though she was upset, it was for her growth. Somehow I still felt uneasy so she reassured me several times that she was OK.

Our days of talking turned into months. I didn't fully understand how deep her wounds were or how raw, I found myself wishing her pain away. I loved her from the moment we talked, and I don't know the exact moment that she knew she loved me however in our daily conversations I always felt loved. So I would ask her often,
"do you love me?"
and she would often respond,
"quit being nosy"
I don't know this for sure but she seemed to be saving those three words for a special moment. Shawna is not only prolific in her writings and with her words she is also well versed in the needs and desires of women and she knew how much I desired hearing her say those words to me, and I will never forget the night she told them to me. It was as if she knew that whatever reserve I may have had would be diminished in hearing them, and she was right. It's an amazing thing to be intimate with someone who you love and know they love you back.

At times my emotions sat on the edge of my seat riveted by the intensity of her kindness. She said the best things to me, things I never realized I needed to hear and where there was emptiness she completely filled me to the point where nothing was missing, overwhelming an empty feeling that had become my bed mate at night and my shadow during the day.

Our conversations would build to the height of extravagant intimacy, and we eventually had romantic encounters that only exploded my desire to be with her more, at times I found myself wanting her to be my spouse.

I experienced a lot of first times with her, like the first time she kissed me was unforgettable. I had never been kissed by anyone in a way that it lingered. Even days later after she kissed me I remember being in between the state of dreaming and not fully awake feeling her kiss still with me, things that were dormant in me that I thought were dead all of sudden began to yawn, wake up and pursue space inside my heart.

I often wondered if this relationship could be real, can someone really love me this much and I know it as real. She made me laugh a lot and cry a lot and equally I tried my best to make her smile which wasn't hard because she smiled and laughed all the time. Sometimes it seemed the whole world lit up when she smiled and it would be just us two around. Through the good there were also times that I made her sad and we misunderstood each other. In those times she had an amazing gift to communicate and pursue a better understanding or as she said once, "we need to talk until we have a GREAT understanding". I admired this quality in her to exude such strength for our relationship while trusting her God to maintain her fragility. I never expected to become so emotionally attached to Shawna but I did and that's what made things hard because in deep relationships both people expect things and when those expectations aren't met you become disappointed...I know I disappointed her a few times.

I experienced with her something that although at times complicated was also very sincere and better than most relationships I have ever known.

I will always 'cherish' what we were.

LTBT II-CONFESSIONS

LTBT II-CONFESSIONS

Confession #5

How we met: At the hotel in suburban lodge, one night after I got pulled over. We had a mutual friend named Donny which I was his at the time.

Our friendship: She had business at this particular hotel but sometimes her visits weren't always business! We began to talk as friends, talking about the dissolving relationship between myself Donny and her and her girlfriend. We were both taking care of children that weren't ours. We were both hustlers, two different kinds and we both are cancers and had the same view on a lot of things. We had a lot in common so it was a good fit.

Our relationship: It just kind of naturally happened, I had the biggest crush on her but knew she had a girlfriend, so I didn't know how to express my feelings since dating women was new to me. I didn't know how to act with these new emotions I was experiencing. I didn't know how people would react to someone who freely expressed their homosexuality. But I had an admiration for her free spirit. It was enticing like a drug, if you would say. I had never met someone who was so attentive. And from nowhere me and my ex had an awful breakup, (you know baby mama drama) so I moved in with my best friend. Her boyfriend was singing at this honky-tonk lounge/bar so that night I was determined to express the way I felt. I bought her roses and we were the only female couple on the dance floor, it was euphoric. Needless to say we got kicked out of the lounge/bar. I was sitting on her lap when a lady came over in her so country dialect, "we don't do that sorta thing in here, so you're gonna hafta leave".
Even though everyone had our back, we were clowning on the way back. That was the reminisce of our first real date. From that date I knew that being with her regardless of what others thought was what I wanted. I gained the confidence quickly to come out to my family and friends (and anyone who listen).

The Demise: We kicked it for months and I was ok with the fact of the other woman. Because she spent the majority of her time with me until I went to work. But one thing about Shawna is she is beautiful and she knows it so therefore she is a flirt by nature. So it got out of control. She started cheating on me with one of my co-workers. I could not handle that it was too much. I already had to compete with someone she was in love with. I find myself falling in love with her so I couldn't take sharing that feeling with anyone else. At the time me and her cousin were friends, so she disclosed some of Shawna's secrets that she didn't want revealed. Or so that gave me great alarm and on top of my jealousy I called and let her girlfriend know what was going on. It didn't go the way I thought so there it was, the end of Micah and Shawna.

The Recovery!: A few months went by and of course I was missing Shawna, and it was killing me she acted like we never happened. So I paged her (lmbo-aint that ancient). We met we talked and what I realize was when you have a love that genuine that is so real that you feel it down to your soul. You just can't let that go. Do I love Shawna ABSOLUTELY! UNDOUBTEDLY! Can we ever be a couple again? No! but what I learned and receive from Shawna is priceless. I love my beautiful friend! That's why to this day I'm proud to say Shawna Monique Harrison is indeed my friend! (FYI I met Shawna when I was 22 and I'm now 33 you do the math, I love you Shawna!! **MUAHH!!**)

LTTBT II-CONFESSIONS

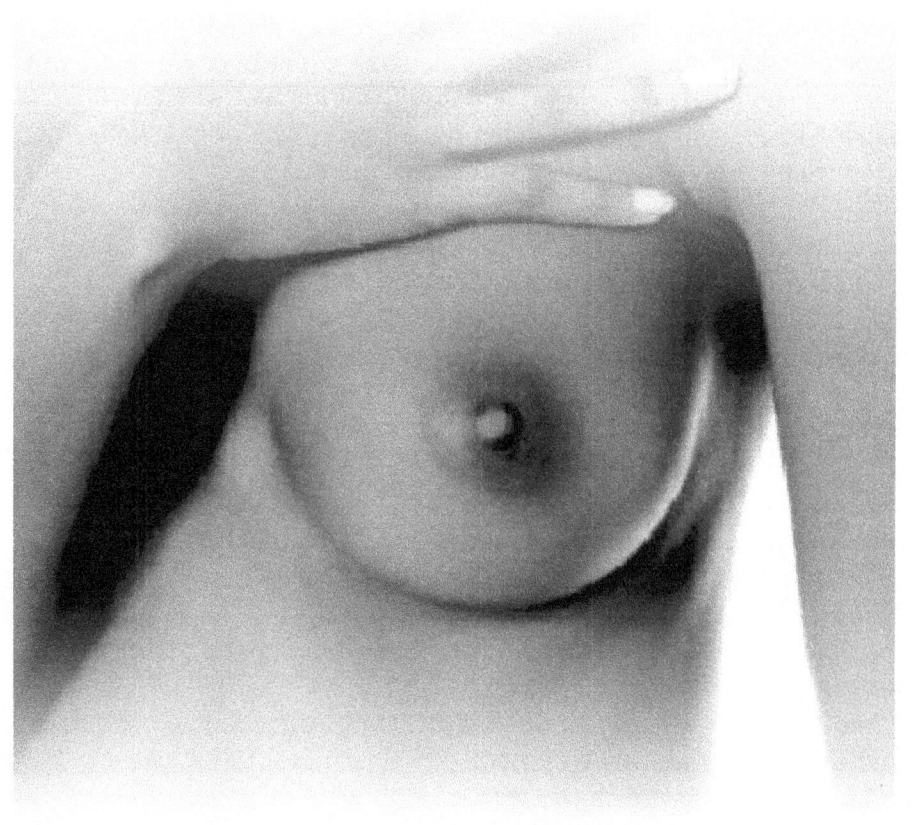

Confession #6

I knew she existed but I didn't know who she was. Years of knowing of her pondered my mind. I couldn't wait to meet and greet this stranger that would change my life tremendously.

As I daydream about the rumors, lies, and stories that were told to me that made me think differently of her. The day the number was told to me sent a shock of relief through my body. Finally I would talk to the monster that everyone made her to be. She would soon talk to me on the phone. When the phone ring it would seem like forever with each ring made my heart skip a beat. I'm nervous, I'm sweating and wondering if this monster would accept me for who I am or would she try to take over my life my soul and manipulate my mind. The voice that I thought was a monster sounded like an innocent bystander in a drive by. The woman on the phone introduced herself and I replied with a "hey how are you?".

The conversation that I thought would last for a second turned into hours of laughter and playing catch up like we knew each other for years. That night turned into months of nonstop talking from 11 to 7 as we both were working the job we would stay up for hours laughing and joking about any and everything whether it was name that movie or name that song, we would text all day and send pics on the low.

The conversations were harmless but it was sure enough hurting our significant others. My husband complained and her lover envied me but we ignored them as if they weren't apart of our lives.

One night turned into two and before we knew it we were planning our first trip to see each other.
As the 45 degree weather hit my caramel complexion face we stood in front of the bus station as we embraced one another. The female I talked to for over six months now had a face. I didn't want to let go because in my mind we were connected. She looked prettier in person than the pics on my phone. Her teeth was so white and her hair was messy and short but she rocked it. I didn't want to let go because she was my new found friend as we look each other up and down both of our smiles were made of gold.

She was 4 ft 11 just like I imagine, and she was well proportioned just like I imagined, she was very pretty.

I picked her bags up off the ground and carried them to the car that was pulled along the sidewalk which I had my flashes on. She opened the car door and that was unexpected but she kind of intimidated me knowing I let a female open my door. In my mind that was abnormal in her world perfect lady.
I said, "thank you."
She replied, "you welcome baby".
I gave a thumbs up and she gave a smile. We hopped in the car and slammed the door. I turned up the music that was on pause we both bobbed our heads to the R & B sound of Kenny Latimore. I was singing every note and she was staring at me like she like it, she nudged my arm and we both busted out laughing. We started to reminisce about the conversations on the phone. We arrived shortly at my house that was full of toys in the yard, the grass was kind of high, she made a couple of jokes about my grass then we went inside.

I introduced her to my kids and my husband, she replied, "what's up blackman?" My husband gave her a warm welcome with a hug, then I took her bags down the hall. She got settled in. She told me she was starving. We went and ate at Texas Roadhouse, we dined in we talked for awhile and right then and there we had so much in common.

We decided to hit the town that night with a couple of my girlfriends. We had a ball they enjoyed her, (life of the party) and her sarcastic way, we danced, she drank, I laughed, she partied. We left the club at 3:30 am. Heading home, my husband was gone when we arrived she hopped in the shower with a towel wrapped around her waist. Her perky titties stood still like a model.
I giggled when she walked in my room.
She replied, "what?".
I replied, "Put some clothes on".
We both laughed, she proceeded in the room across the hall.

LTTBT II-CONFESSIONS

I laid in my bed thinking about the whole day I encountered with my new friend and it was nice.

The voice in the other room kept yelling, "Are you sleep?"
and I would reply, "go to bed".
I have never been around a lesbian before, so I was kind of scared. 30 minutes went by and my new found friend was standing in my doorway telling me that she couldn't sleep. I was nervous because this isn't normal. I was nervous and my palms were sweaty, she asked if she could lay with me and I replied, "yes". We faced each other and she whispered, "are you scared of a gay woman laying in your bed?" And I said, "a little bit" she assured me that it was okay and that I could ask her anything that was on my mind. I ask numerous of questions and she answered every one to the best of her knowledge and for once in my life face to face with my new friend I didn't want this night to end. From that moment on my friend was visiting me like I was her woman, every other month we kicked it hard going out hanging with my friends they treated her like she was a celebrity but as long as we kicked it nothing else mattered to me not even our lovers.

On the inside I felt nasty but on the outside I love every bit of her. I remember like it was yesterday the first time she leaned in and we shared a passionate kiss, a part of me wanted to pull away because I have never touched a female before but I couldn't move I felt like I was in love at first sight. My emotions were mixed up. What if my husband catches us what would he do? Would her lover approve of this behavior? We couldn't stop being special friends, nights I would cry to myself that this was wrong and what would people think of me but when we seen each other it was all about me and her.

I went to visit her with a couple of friends and I had never met her lover in person. She told us we could crash at her house and at first I was nervous but f**** that she was my friend. Her nephew greeted us at the door with open arms and her lover stayed in the room, we put our bags down and she showed us her apartment, and animals. She led us down what seemed like a long hallway but in all honesty I didn't want to meet what was behind

door number one. As she opened the door this thin light skinned girl raised up and gave us a look that could kill. We spoke to show respect, and she gave us a "how ya doing, my name is Melanie".
She cracked a smile, we then gave a slight grin back. I knew she hated me and I felt awkward in her house knowing she had the trophy and I only had a small prize. We got settled in, we shot the breeze in the living room with her nephew and her, laughing, joking and playing tricks on each other.

We left and she introduced me to her younger brother, a wannabe gangsta that didn't thrill us at all. He had beautiful children and his girlfriend was a small framed chic who seemed like she was afraid of him. That night we played cards and joked around until about 3 a.m.

Shawna made our pallets on the floor and told us we had to be quiet because her lover was sleeping. We giggled a little bit but inside I was boiling. My friends and I agreed and she went in her room and never came back out. My feelings were hurt but how could I be mad I was married and that was her girl. Later on that night I could hear moans and groans coming from the next door. I was sick to my stomach, I couldn't sleep I tossed and turned all night knowing that SH** was popping off and she had no respect for me. The next morning Shawna said, "good morning" which I was nonchalant with a slight attitude. Shawna knew I was mad she kissed my a** the whole day but I didn't care because the only thing I could think about was the sounds coming from the room last night. She bought me dinner and opened up the car doors trying to plead her case as if she was on trial and I was her judge. The look in her eyes made me melt, this woman had me right where she wanted me and I was hook by her charm. That night we went out, she was like a celebrity on the red carpet. In the club there was women hugging and kissing my girl but the jealous person I am didn't show a bit of jealousy. We danced, we grind, and even laughed on the dance floor. I was high on life with her, nothing was coming in between me and Shawna. We were two peas in a pod, I didn't want this weekend to end.

The next morning we packed and I said my good byes to Shawna. We embraced and on the low gave each other a brisk kiss, which I thought would be on the cheek but instead her lips locked mine and for the first time in my life I kissed a woman and loved it. Tears rolled down my face and she ask me if I was okay. I replied, "yes, I'm fine" and I left her standing in the driveway and I waved until I couldn't see her any longer.

The ride home was hard, thoughts kept going through my mind.
My husband?
Shawna?
What am I going to do?
Why do I feel this way?
This sh** couldn't be normal. My phone suddenly had a text going across the screen that read,
"Are you at home? Are you ok?"
I replied, "Yes."
I got home kissed my husband, made love to him, he kissed and played every inch of my body. As he kissed my honey pot when he looked up at me I seen Shawna and it was scary, "why me God?" Please send me a sign. I had to know what I was getting myself into, from kissing, touching and tasting this woman I was in love and I knew she wanted me too. We cried, laughed, talked and on the outside she was mine but on the inside I knew it would never be.

We were in two separate worlds, I loved Shawna and I was willing to open up but as months and even a year went by Shawna changed. The calls got short and the visits became shorter. We started to disagree on everything, the phone calls that were once all night became one to two hours tops. But the day Shawna told me she met another woman and she was into church I knew then that all her time was being spent with this new woman.

I was hurt and I felt betrayed. I confronted her on how I felt. Then I got the shock of my life when the woman that I felt was more than just a friend told me that I shouldn't be mad because we weren't together. I wanted to bash her face in and leave her hurt and crying like she made me but the person I know I am couldn't be that way. No wonder she hasn't been answering my calls or showing me affection because Shawna has been spending all her time with this other mystery woman. My heart was cold I hated Shawna and she knew it. The next couple of months were hard for me. I had to start my closing process with Shawna. I wanted to keep her as my friend but not as my secret lover.

As the months progressed my feelings for Shawna grew weak and distant, I took all my pain and hurt and turned it into a positive. I refuse to let this beat me I'm much stronger now. I love Shawna but I'm not in love with Shawna. She opened up a lot of doors that I thought I never had and showed me an experience that never would have happened if I hadn't met Shawna, the woman. The person I am today is different from who I was a couple years ago.

I have learned the power, struggle, and life of being with a gay woman on the low. And if I knew we could make it together she would have been the woman I would marry, not a man. Shawna and I are very close and I wouldn't give that up for the world.

She put the 'F' in Friends are Forever!

LTTBT II-CONFESSIONS

Confession #7

It was the usual slow day at my job. I was so bored I was finding things to do. All of a sudden I see this very pretty light skinned girl with a cowboy hat on. She was dressed very different from anybody that I have ever met. She began to walk right past me until she realized that I was eyeballing her up and down. She turned back around and needed my help to find something.

As she began walking closer to me, I didn't know what to do but try to smile and be nice. She introduced herself as Ms. Shawna Harrison, and I told her who I was. We had a brief conversation about her attire because I thought it was cute and artistic. She had a great personality and never took offense to anything that I said. But it was something about her that made me want to become closer to her. Out of all the days that I felt worthless and useless to the world, that went away the minute I saw her. The way she carried herself as a woman, made me want to go down the same positive path.

She began to tell me that she was a writer and that she wanted me to read her writings. I was very honored that she asked me to read some of the things she wrote, at that moment she didn't have any with her but that was my chance to see her again. As she began to leave my place of employment, I couldn't stop thinking about her. When she left I knew she would be back shortly, so I went to go to the rest room to make sure my hair was combed, my breath was fresh, and that I had on enough lip gloss to last all day. You would have thought I was going on a date but I wanted to make a second good impression on her.

As she arrived back she had her writings in hand and it seemed like she was excited to share the things she wrote with me. I received the writings and told her that I will let her know what I thought about them after I read them. We talked briefly and exchanged numbers. Two or three days later, I called her and we talked about her writings. I expressed my feelings and told her that I was so sorry for all the pain that she endured. I would have never thought that someone would do any harm to such a beautiful person.

Days went by and we didn't have any contact over the phone but we always seemed to run into each other everyday. I wanted to get to know her, but I didn't know what to say. I dreamed about her for two days straight and when I saw her my mind went blank. When we would have brief conversations, we would laugh and joke around so I didn't know when I should be serious.

At one point I thought I was crazy, but I was infatuated with what I saw, and what I didn't know about her. I just wanted to be a part of her life (at least three times a week because that's how often I would see her at work) and I would be happy. I just wanted someone to show me how to love myself and be a good friend to me. I never thought in a million years that it would be Ms. Shawna Harrison. At this point in my life I was tired of being used and abused in relationships that I thought were going to change (eventually). I wanted to be loved, and I only wanted it from her. I just wanted the joy that she appeared to have that I didn't. After reading her writings I knew that she lived her life as a lesbian, and I was bisexual. So I didn't think it would ever work between us.

As time went on I began to see her and her son more often than usual. I have an eight year old son and when I did see her they would play and we would talk. After a few months of getting to know each other, I asked her if it would be okay for me to come and get her son sometime to play with my son. She didn't feel comfortable with that so she decided that he could play with him but only under her conditions. So they would see each other at least three to four times a week. I was happy with the boys getting along but most importantly, I had the chance to be around her and get to see her a lot. Once we began to get closer to one another, we formed a strong friendship. We started doing things with the children together, such as: going out to eat, taking them to the park, or just chilling watching a movie.

I think I had more fun than the children. I never had anyone care for me and my child like that in a long time. She was there for me, and I was loving every minute of her loving spirit. She would always make me smile and laugh even when I wasn't in the mood. She grew on me so quickly. As days passed by we decided that we wanted more than just a friendship. But

it wasn't going to be as easy as I thought it would be. It took me at least three months just to get a damn kiss (can you believe that?) All I can say is that it was worth the wait.

Our first kiss was the best kiss I have ever had in my life. It was so soft, wet, and sensual all at the same time. I felt so free with myself, and I knew she felt the same way. But that was as far as it went for a long time. I wanted more but I had to wait until she was ready. I was so anxious but I had no idea what I was getting myself into.

The next day Shawna invited me over for dinner. Me and my son went over later that night. We ate, watched TV, and talked about whatever we were feeling that day. After two or three hours had passed, I was invited to stay the night. I didn't bring anything that I needed so I had to make a quick trip back home. I was so excited that half of the things I needed got left behind. When I returned she was already ready for bed. I was so nervous, that my hands were sweating. By the time I got back the kids were in the bed going to sleep.

We began kissing each other as soon as we got to the bedroom door. The nervousness finally went away. I felt like no one would ever make me feel the way she did that night. We made love for hours, we had a bond like no other bond. As I lay in the bed she rubbed my head very slowly as we kissed like it was our last kiss. Her lips were like sugar to me. I just couldn't get enough. From that moment I knew I would always want to be in Shawna's life and it was not about the wonderful sex we had, it was about being able to express myself without being judged for anything. It became so clear to me that I was dealing with a mature woman that knew what she wanted.

The next morning she cooked me breakfast, iron my clothes, and washed my body when I took a shower. I felt so good about where our relationship was headed. We never talked about being in a serious relationship, but I knew we were committed to each other. We began seeing each other on a regular basis. At the time I was only working a part time job. So I would watch the kids while she worked a twelve hour shift. Some would consider it babysitting, but I considered it a privilege to be a part of her life and her sons life. Her son is a very well mannered young man who was always a great influence on how to be a great child to my son and they played well together.

I felt great about our friendship/lover because for a long time I didn't trust anybody to come into my life and show me that there is a lot of positive things to be grateful for. I became overwhelmed with the love and attention I was getting from Shawna. I was scared that if I let someone in, I would always get hurt like I did in the past. So some days I would start arguments over anything just so I would be able to push myself away and be alone. I never thought about how it would affect the children's friendship. I was so use to being alone and not having any friends that cared about me until I met the one that loved me very much. But I didn't know how to appreciate it.

Shawna stayed by my side through the good and the bad. Some days I would be mad about things that happened at work, or my son would do something to make me upset with him, but she was always there, no matter how much I got on her nerves. I never really saw her show herself being stressed out about anything, she was so comforting for me. And some days I would sit in my bedroom and cry because I knew that she is suppose to be in my life. I was so caught up on my own BS I was destroying our friendship quickly she would try to make it work, and I would mess it back up, until one day we decided to take a break from each other, but we would let the kids see each other, occasionally. Weeks passed by and we didn't call each other at all. I missed her so much. By then I was so in love with her, I was going crazy in my mind. I knew I f***** up that's why I just prayed that God would fix things. But it wasn't just all on God. I needed to fix my attitude on life and deal with my issues head on. But I didn't hear from Shawna for about another month or two I was worried that she had given up on me.

I think that Shawna and I needed more time to build a great friendship to where we weren't having sex with one another. I wanted her and her friendship more than anything in the whole world and I would have gave anything and everything to be a part of her life again. I love her so so much, but I didn't show her enough and I wasn't there for her as a strong friend that she wanted from me I finally got the chance to talk to her when she decided to call me. I was so excited and happy that I didn't even answer the phone I waited for a minute and called her back. We talked and I wanted to apologize for my actions but she told me that she wanted to talk in person. I was hesitant because I didn't know how we would interact with each other after all this time. I went to her house, me and my son that afternoon. We talked but the conversation was not the same. I apologize for everything and told her how much I missed her. Being the good person that Shawna is, she told me that she forgave me and that she wanted us to become friends again. I knew that this was my chance to be the friend she knew I could be we have been friends ever since. But everything is not peaches and cream always.

We still have our ups and downs but Shawna will always be the best friend I have ever had. And our children still play with each other.

EPILOGUE

Confession 1
I appreciate your thoughts, your words, your honesty. I will forever be your friend.

Confession 2
I remember coming up and hanging with you at your job and the first date we went on was at the mall, I was so nervous but very confident in knowing that at that moment with you was where I wanted to be. Know that you made me smile in a way that others didn't. Thank you I love you.

Confession 3
You have been the second and last woman in the whole world that I have expressed, trusted and felt totally comfortable with. My heart hurts in a good way just from the amount of love I have for you.

Confession 4
You have showed your love for me not once, not twice but continuously. Thank you for depositing goodness in me. I love you.

Confession 5
Look at where we were and where we are now. We have over 10 years under our belt. I love you then, I really love you now.

Confession 6
Our friendship grew way beyond what we ever imagined. Our bond will never die. I'm sorry for hurting you. Love you dude.

Confession 7
Thank you for trusting yourself with me. I know it was challenging to open up. You have a huge heart, I'm grateful that you shared it with me. I love you.

For the women that chose not to share our story because they didn't want the world to know cause our story is too special/intimate, because it's too hard to relive all those emotions again.

I understand, that doesn't diminish or alter my love, respect, compassion, and appreciation for you. Thank you for impacting my life.
I love you!

RESOURCES

Exodus International
www.exodusinternational.org

Exodus is a non profit, interdenominational christian organization promoting the message of freedom from homosexuality through the power of Jesus Christ.

Joseph Coat Ministries
www.josephcoatministries.com

Is change possible? Joseph Coat Ministries affirms that reorientation of homosexuality/same sex attraction is possible. This is a process that begins with motivation and self determination to change based upon a personal relationship with Jesus Christ.

Cross Ministry
www.crossministry.org

FirstStone Ministry
www.firststone.org

Leading people in the body of Christ to freedom from homosexuality and sexual brokenness through Jesus Christ.

Parents and Friends of Ex Gays
www.pfox.org

PFOX is a national non profit organization that support families, advocates for the ex gay community and educates the public on sexual orientation. Works to eliminate negative perceptions and discrimination against former homosexuals.

LET THE TRUTH BE TOLD II
Confessions

To contact the author for more information, to order more books, to book for speaking engagements or to publish your own books, go to her website:
www.shawnaharrison.com

or email her at:
shawna_mytruesoul@yahoo.com

LTTBT II-CONFESSIONS

www.ingramcontent.com/pod-product-compliance
Lightning Source LLC
LaVergne TN
LVHW011430080426
835512LV00005B/372